# Mammal Babies

Catherine Veitch

Raintree

Raintree is an imprint of Capstone Global Library Limited,
a company incorporated in England and Wales having its
registered office at 7 Pilgrim Street, London, EC4V 6LB –
Registered company number: 6695582

To contact Raintree:
Phone: 0845 6044371
Fax: + 44 (0) 1865 312263
Email: myorders@raintreepublishers.co.uk
Outside the UK please telephone +44 1865 312262.

Text © Capstone Global Library Limited 2013
First published in hardback in 2013
The moral rights of the proprietor have been asserted.

Edited by Daniel Nunn, Rebecca Rissman,
and Catherine Veitch
Designed by Cynthia Della-Rovere
Picture research by Ruth Blair
Production by Victoria Fitzgerald
Originated by Capstone Global Library
Printed and bound in China

ISBN 978 1 406 25925 4
17 16 15 14 13
10 9 8 7 6 5 4 3 2 1

**British Library Cataloguing in Publication Data**
Veitch, Catherine.
Mammal babies. -- (Animal babies)
599.1'39-dc23
A full catalogue record for this book is available from the
British Library.

**Acknowledgements**
We would like to thank the following for permission to
reproduce photographs: Corbis p. 10 (© Jenny E. Ross),
19 (© Tim Fitzharris/Minden Pictures); Getty Images pp.
11 (Aurora), 12 (Sumio Harada/Minden Pictures), 15
(Oxford Scientific) 23 (Oxford Scientific); Naturepl pp.5
(© Anup Shah), 6 (© Jane Burton), 7 (© Eric Baccega);
13 (© Steven David Miller), 16 (© Peter Blackwell), 17
(© Anup Shah), 23 (© Anup Shah); Shutterstock pp.
title page (© Villiers Steyn), 4 (© Joel Shawn), 8 (©
holbox), 9 (© Villiers Steyn), 14 (© Krzysztof Wiktor), 18
(© Lenkadan), 20 (© Kati Molin), 21 (© Flashon Studio),
22 (© Uryadnikov Sergey, © Kitch Bain), 23 (© Flashon
Studio).

Front cover photograph of a Bornean orangutan cuddling
her baby reproduced with kind permission of Corbis
(© Anup Shah).

We would like to thank Michael Bright for his invaluable
help in the preparation of this book.

Every effort has been made to contact copyright holders
of material reproduced in this book. Any omissions will
be rectified in subsequent printings if notice is given to
the publisher.

# Contents

# What is a mammal?

hair

A mammal is an animal with hair or fur.

Female mammals feed their babies milk.

# How are baby mammals born?

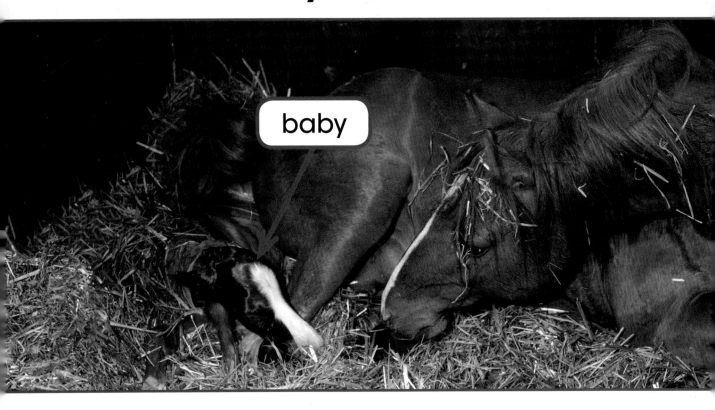

baby

Most female mammals give birth
to babies.

Some mammals have one baby at a time.

Some mammals have many babies at a time.

Most baby mammals look like
their parents.

# Where do baby mammals live?

den

Baby mammals need a safe place to live. Many baby mammals live in dens.

burrow

Many baby mammals live in burrows.

nest

Many baby mammals live in nests.

pouch

Some baby mammals live in their mothers' pouches.

# Caring for baby mammals

Many mammals lick their babies' fur to keep it clean.

Many mammals protect their babies from predators.

Many mammals teach their babies to hunt.

Many mammals teach their babies
to fight.

Many mammal babies stay with their mothers for a long time.

Some mammals are looked after
by both parents.

Humans are mammals, too.

Human babies need a lot of help
from adults.

# Life cycle of a mammal

baby
orang-utan

adult
orang-utan

young
orang-utan

A life cycle shows the different stages of an animal's life. This is the life cycle of an orang-utan.

# Picture glossary

**adult** grown-up. A child grows into an adult.

**female** animal that can give birth. Female mammals feed their babies milk from their bodies.

**predator** animal that eats other animals

# Index

**Notes for parents and teachers**

**Before reading**

Show children a collection of photos and videos of mammals. National Geographic and BBC Nature are useful websites. Explain what a mammal is and discuss the characteristics of mammals.

**After reading**

- Mount photos of adult and baby mammals on card, and play games of snap and pairs where the children have to match a baby mammal with its parent. Model the correct pairs first.

- Ask children to label the parts of a mammal: for example, fur, legs, tail, ears.

- Look at page 22 and discuss the life cycle stages of a mammal. Mount photos of the baby, young and adult stages and ask children to put the photos in order. Encourage children to draw a life cycle of a human to compare. Compare how different mammals care for their babies. Discuss the care human babies need.

- To extend children's knowledge, the mammals are as follows: zebra: p4; impala and fawn: p5; horse and foal: p6; seal and pup: p7; dog and puppies: p8; elephant and calf: p9; polar bear cubs: p10; kittens (baby rabbits): p11; kittens (baby squirrels): p12; kangaroo and joey: p13; lioness and cub: p14; bear and cubs: p15; cheetah and cub: p16; infant baboons: p17; horse and foal: p18; wolves and cub: p19.